THIS IS THE STORY OF JAMES EARL CARTER JR., THE 39TH PRESIDENT OF THE UNITED STATES.

A MAVERICK STATESMAN, ILL-SUITED FOR THE EGO DRIVEN POLITICAL GAMES WHICH DEFINE WASHINGTON POLITICS.

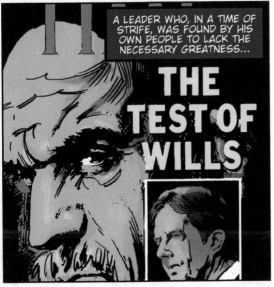

A LEADER WHO, IN A TIME OF STRIFE, WAS FOUND BY HIS OWN PEOPLE TO LACK THE NECESSARY GREATNESS...

THE TEST OF WILLS

...AND WAS UNFORTUNATE ENOUGH TO BE FACING STRONG RIVALS ON BOTH SIDES.

PERHAPS MOST IMPORTANTLY, THIS IS THE TALE OF A MAN WHO ROSE FROM THE ASHES OF A FAILED PRESIDENCY TO OUTSHINE WHAT MOST IN THE EXECUTIVE OFFICE WOULD EVER ACCOMPLISH.

ON OCTOBER 1ST, 1924, JIMMY CARTER WAS BORN IN PLAINS, GEORGIA.

CARTER WAS BORN INTO A SUCCESSFUL, SOUTHERN FAMILY. JAMES SR. WAS A FARMER, LANDOWNER, AND ENTREPRENEUR. BESSIE, HIS MOTHER, WAS A NURSE BY TRADE.

JIMMY WAS MILD-MANNERED AND STUDIOUS AS A CHILD. HE DID WHATEVER HE WAS CAPABLE OF TO HELP HIS PARENTS ON THE FARM AND TO ABSORB ANY KNOWLEDGE HE COULD.

THE CARTERS WERE DEEPLY RELIGIOUS FOLKS, WITH PROGRESSIVE VIEWS ON RACE. MANY OF JIMMY'S EARLY ROLE MODELS WERE AFRICAN AMERICANS.

KIND AND CHARITABLE, THE CARTERS NEVER TURNED AWAY HONEST FOLKS WHO HAD FALLEN ON HARD TIMES.

IN ONE OF THE TOUGHEST ECONOMIC TIMES THE UNITED STATES HAD EVER FACED, THE CARTER FAMILY WAS ABLE TO EMPLOY OVER 200 WORKERS.

IT WAS IN THIS FERTILE SOIL OF HONESTY, HARD WORK AND LOVE FOR MANKIND THAT JIMMY CARTER WOULD GROW INTO MAN HE WOULD BE FOR THE REST OF HIS LIFE.

WHEN THE HARD DAYS OF THE GREAT DEPRESSION HIT, THE CARTERS HAD BEEN STRUCK FAR LESS THAN MOST. THEIR FARM STRIVED AND THEY BECAME KNOWN FOR THEIR GENEROSITY TOWARD MIGRANT WORKERS.

JIMMY CARTER, AT THE AGE OF 17, BECAME THE FIRST PERSON IN HIS FATHER'S FAMILY TO GRADUATE FROM HIGH SCHOOL.

YOUNG JIMMY'S HEART YEARNED TO JOURNEY PAST THE BORDERS OF RURAL GEORGIA AND SEE THE WORLD.

WITH A DESIRE TO SERVE HIS
NATION AND DREAMS OF ADVENTURE
AT SEA, CARTER APPLIED TO THE
NAVAL ACADEMY IN MARYLAND.

AFTER TWO YEARS OF COLLEGE IN
GEORGIA, JIMMY GOT HIS WISH
AND MADE HIS WAY TO MARYLAND.

AT 5'9" AND ONLY 121 POUNDS, CARTER FOUND THE PHYSICAL ASPECTS OF ACADEMY LIFE TO BE PARTICULARLY DIFFICULT.

ALWAYS A BIT INTROVERTED, HIS MIND CONSUMED WITH SPIRITUAL AND INTELLECTUAL PURSUITS, THE FUTURE PRESIDENT OFTEN FOUND HIMSELF THE ODD MAN OUT IN THOSE DAYS.

HIS EARLY NAVY DAYS WERE NOT ALL BAD THOUGH. IT WAS DURING THIS TIME, WHILE HOME ON LEAVE, THAT JIMMY WOULD START DATING HIS SISTER'S SEVENTEEN YEAR OLD FRIEND, ROSALYNN SMITH.

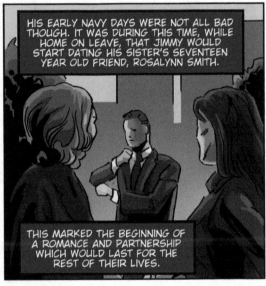

THIS MARKED THE BEGINNING OF A ROMANCE AND PARTNERSHIP WHICH WOULD LAST FOR THE REST OF THEIR LIVES.

DESPITE RESERVATIONS THAT SHE WAS NOT GOOD ENOUGH FOR JIMMY, ROSALYNN AGREED TO MARRY HIM THE VERY NEXT YEAR.

IN 1947, ONE YEAR AFTER THEIR MARRIAGE, THE CARTERS WOULD HAVE THEIR FIRST CHILD, JOHN WILLIAM.

THINGS GOT BETTER IN THE SERVICE AS WELL.

DESPITE ROCKY BEGINNINGS, CARTER WENT ON TO A SUCCESSFUL NAVAL CAREER, EVENTUALLY PREPARING TO SERVE AS ENGINEERING OFFICER ABOARD THE USS SEAWOLF, ONE OF THE FIRST NUCLEAR POWERED SUBMARINES.

IN 1953 HOWEVER, JAMES EARL CARTER SR. DIED OF PANCREATIC CANCER. JIMMY WOULD RETIRE FROM THE NAVY AFTER HIS FATHER'S DEATH, AND TAKE HIS FAMILY HOME TO GEORGIA.

THOUGH HE HAD ENJOYED HIS CAREER AS AN ENGINEER IN THE NAVY, CARTER FOUND COMFORT PLANTING ROOTS BACK INTO HIS HOME SOIL.

OVER THE NEXT EIGHT YEARS CARTER WOULD NOTICE A CULTURAL CHANGE OCCURRING IN THE SOUTH. A PROGRESSIVE ZEITGEIST WAS CORRODING THE WAYS OF THE OLD SOUTH AND USHERING IN A MORE ENLIGHTENED AGE.

THIS KIND OF CULTURAL REBIRTH FILLED JIMMY CARTER WITH THE COURAGE AND CONVICTION TO DIVE HEADLONG INTO THE WORLD OF SOUTHERN POLITICS. IT WOULD NOT BE EASY THOUGH.

CARTER'S FIRST POLITICAL BATTLE WOULD BE AGAINST HOMER MOORE, A CORRUPT AND WELL-CONNECTED POLITICIAN.

HERE, CARTER WOULD WITNESS VOTER FRAUD AND INTIMIDATION FOR THE FIRST TIME.

CARTER WOULD LOSE THE ELECTION, THOUGH HE WOULD FIND THAT 420 BALLOTS WERE CAST WHILE ONLY 333 WERE ISSUED.

THIS FIRST-HAND EXPERIENCE WITH THE OBSTRUCTION OF DEMOCRACY WOULD SHAPE MUCH OF CARTER'S LATER LIFE.

NOT ONE TO SUBMIT TO INJUSTICE, CARTER FOUGHT BACK AGAINST HOMER'S CRIMINAL VICTORY.

AFTER A RECOUNT WAS FINALLY ALLOWED, CARTER FOUND HIMSELF IN THE GEORGIA SENATE.

OVER THE NEXT FOUR YEARS, FROM 1962 THROUGH 1966, CARTER SERVED TWO SUCCESSFUL TERMS IN THE GEORGIA SENATE.

A HARD WORKER, WHO TOOK HIS JOB SERIOUSLY, CARTER READ EVERY BILL WHICH HE VOTED ON.

CARTER AND THEN GOVERNOR CARL SANDERS (SEE VISUAL REFERENCE) WORKED CLOSELY ON SEVERAL ISSUES, INCLUDING GOVERNMENT REFORM.

FOR THIS AND OTHER REASONS, MANY CONSIDERED CARTER TO BE GEORGIA'S MOST EFFECTIVE LEGISLATOR.

IN 1966 JIMMY MADE A RISKY GAMBIT. INSTEAD OF SEEKING A VACANT CONGRESSIONAL SEAT, WHICH WOULD HAVE BEEN AN EASY VICTORY, CARTER RAN FOR GOVERNOR.

THE MODERATE CARTER WOULD LOSE AGAINST A CONSERVATIVE DEMOCRAT NAMED LESTER MADDOX, WHO HAD GAINED SOME NOTORIETY BY DEFYING CIVIL RIGHTS LAWS AND VIOLENTLY FENDING OFF AFRICAN AMERICAN PATRONS TO HIS RESTAURANT.

DISENCHANTED WITH POLITICS, AND DISAPPOINTED IN HOW DISTANT A "NEW SOUTH" SEEMED TO BE, CARTER TURNED HIS ATTENTION TO HIS FARM, TO HIS FAMILY AND TO GOD.

WITH A NEW VIEW ON LIFE AND POLITICS, ONE WHERE POLITICAL POWER COULD BE USED TO BRING DIVINE JUSTICE INTO THE WORLD, CARTER RETURNED TO POLITICS IN 1969.
UNWILLING TO BE DEFEATED AGAIN, JIMMY HIRED AN ENTOURAGE OF CONSULTANTS TO PREPARE HIM FOR THE 1970 ELECTION.
GEORGIA LAW PROHIBITED CONSECUTIVE GUBERNATORIAL TERMS. WITH MADDOX ON HIS WAY OUT, THE DEMOCRATIC PRIMARY WOULD BE FOUGHT BETWEEN CARTER AND HIS ONE-TIME ALLY AND FORMER GOVERNOR , CARL SANDERS.
BOTH MEN WERE PROGRESSIVE SOUTHERNERS. THEIR SIMILARITIES WORKED AS A DISADVANTAGE TO THE LESS EXPERIENCED CARTER WHO SEEMED TO BRING NOTHING TO THE TABLE THAT SANDERS DIDN'T AS WELL.
CARTER AND HIS TEAM RELIED ON THE TACTIC OF PAINTING SANDERS AS A RUSTY COG IN A CORRUPT MACHINE. IN CONTRAST, THE FORMER SENATOR POSITIONED HIMSELF AS A POLITICAL OUTSIDER WHO WOULD STRAIGHTEN OUT THE GOVERNMENT.
CARTER'S CAMPAIGN ALSO UTILIZED RACE BAITING TACTICS TO PAINT THE FORMER GOVERNOR AS RADICAL LIBERAL IN CAHOOTS WITH THE MISTRUSTED FEDERAL GOVERNMENT.
CARTER CAMPAIGN
WEATHER
Fair and cooler. National summary on Page 12B
Vol. 94, No. 209
FINAL
HOME EDITION
Price 15 Cents
Price May Be Higher Outside Retail Trading Zone
THE DIRTY AND UNCOUTH CAMPAIGN THAT CARTER RAN EARNED HIM THE LIFE-LONG IRE OF HIS FORMER POLITICAL ALLY. SANDERS WOULD REFER TO CARTER AS THE "PENNY-ANTIEST POLITICIAN I'VE EVER COME ACROSS".
CARTER WINS
'Was a Good Two Years,' Winner Says
By ANDREW MOLLISON And ANDREW GLASS
THE SHREWD, IF IN-ADMIRABLE, TACTICS OF THE CARTER CAMPAIGN PROVED SUCCESSFUL. JIMMY CARTER WOULD DEFEAT SANDERS IN THE PRIMARIES AND GO TO BE ELECTED AS THE GOVERNOR OF GEORGIA.
Jimmy Carter (D)
Gerald Ford (R)
Eugene McCarthy (Ind.)
Lester Maddox (AIP)
3rd District Congress

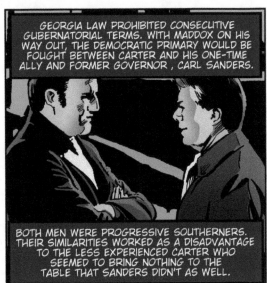

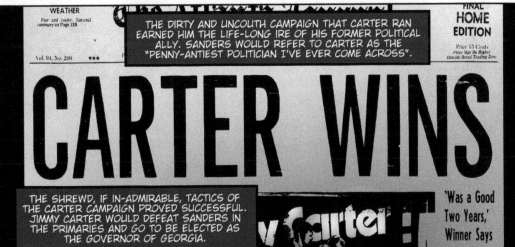

ONCE IN OFFICE, JIMMY WOULD MAINTAIN HIS OUTSIDER PERSONA. IN LIEU OF SPENDING TAX PAYER'S MONEY ON EXPENSIVE POLITICAL PARTIES, HE WOULD INVITE LEGISLATORS TO DINE ON MORE MODEST FARE.

IN MANY WAYS, THIS DISREGARD OF POLITICAL PROTOCOL WOULD SHAPE BOTH HIS FUTURE SUCCESSES AND FAILURES.

CARTER WOULD MAKE GOOD ON HIS PROMISES TO CLEAN UP THE GOVERNMENT AND LIMIT EXCESSIVE SPENDING. HIS ADMINISTRATION WOULD INSTATE NEW BUDGET POLICIES THAT CUT GREATLY DOWN ON FINANCIAL WASTE.

WHILE PUBLICLY SKIRTING AROUND THE ISSUE OF RACE, CARTER DID QUIETLY INCREASE THE NUMBER OF HIGH RANKING GOVERNMENT POSITIONS HELD BY BLACK PEOPLE IN GEORGIA.

CARTER WOULD EVEN HOLD "SPEAK UP DAYS", WHERE THE STATE'S CITIZENS WERE WELCOME TO BRING THEIR PROBLEMS STRAIGHT TO THE GOVERNOR.

CARTER EVEN PROVED TO BE A MAN THAT COULD ADMIT HIS MISTAKES.

AFTER LEARNING THAT A DAM BUILDING PROJECT WHICH HE HAD GIVEN THE GO AHEAD TO WOULD HAVE NEGATIVE ENVIRONMENTAL EFFECTS, HE WORKED TO SHUT DOWN THE PROJECT FOR GOOD.

BY 1972, CARTER'S AMBITIONS HAD GROWN AND HIS GAZE TURNED TOWARD THE WHITE HOUSE.

THE WATERGATE SCANDAL HAD LEFT WASHINGTON'S POLITICAL LANDSCAPE FERTILE FOR A CHANGE OF PARTY.

FURTHERMORE, PEOPLE'S DISTRUST IN THE GOVERNMENT AT LARGE PROVIDED PERFECT TIMING FOR AN OUTSIDER- A MAVERICK POLITICIAN- TO MAKE A BID FOR THE PRESIDENCY.

A NATURAL ON CAMERA, CARTER'S SMILE AND CHARISMA MADE FOR GOOD TELEVISION. THE FUTURE PRESIDENT MADE GOOD USE OF THE MEDIA'S FANCY WITH HIM TO STRENGTHEN HIS CAMPAIGN.

Why One Man Is Optimistic About America's Third Century

Jimmy Carter

CARTER'S CAMPAIGN EMPLOYED UNUSUAL TACTICS, COURTING FAVOR FROM OVERLOOKED STATES, AND PUBLISHING AN AUTOBIOGRAPHY TO DEMONSTRATE HE WAS A PEOPLE'S STATESMAN, RATHER THAN AN ESTABLISHMENT CRONY.

OF COURSE THE GOVERNOR'S MAVERICK STANCE GARNERED NEGATIVE ATTENTION AS WELL. WRITER, STEN BRILL CHARACTERIZED CARTER AS "A VERY SMART, HARD-WORKING, TOUGH POLITICIAN WHO'S CAMPAIGNING AS AN ANTI- POLITICIAN."

JIMMY CARTER'S PATHETIC LIES

DESPITE THOSE WHO FELT CARTER TO BE DISINGENUOUS, THE GEORGIA GOVERNOR WAS ABLE TO LEAD THE SPLINTERED DEMOCRATIC PARTY TO VICTORY OVER A DISGRACED GOP.

MORE IMPORTANTLY, THIS NEW PRESIDENT OF THE UNITED STATES GAVE THE PEOPLE A SENSE OF CHANGE AND OF HOPE. SADLY IT WOULDN'T LAST FOR LONG.

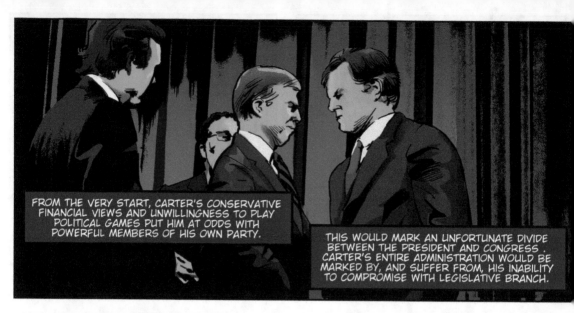

FROM THE VERY START, CARTER'S CONSERVATIVE FINANCIAL VIEWS AND UNWILLINGNESS TO PLAY POLITICAL GAMES PUT HIM AT ODDS WITH POWERFUL MEMBERS OF HIS OWN PARTY.

THIS WOULD MARK AN UNFORTUNATE DIVIDE BETWEEN THE PRESIDENT AND CONGRESS. CARTER'S ENTIRE ADMINISTRATION WOULD BE MARKED BY, AND SUFFER FROM, HIS INABILITY TO COMPROMISE WITH LEGISLATIVE BRANCH.

THE ENERGY CRISIS REQUIRES PAINFUL SACRIFICES. WHAT IS NEEDED WILL BE THE MORAL EQUIVALENT OF WAR.

HAVING LITTLE LUCK WITH THE WASHINGTON INSIDERS, THE MAVERICK PRESIDENT HOPED TO ENLIST SUPPORT OF THE PEOPLE TO PUSH HIS MORE PROGRESSIVE AGENDAS THROUGH.

THIS TACTIC WORKED, AT LEAST SOMEWHAT. CARTER'S ENERGY BILL WAS PASSED, THOUGH CONGRESS HAD STRIPPED IT TO ITS BARE BONES.

ANOTHER OF THE PRESIDENT'S GREATEST VICTORIES WOULD DEFINE HIM, FOR THE REST OF HIS LIFE.

THE CAMP DAVID ACCORDS WERE, BY CARTER'S OWN ACCOUNT, THE PARAMOUNT MOMENT OF HIS PRESIDENCY.

FOR 13 DAYS CARTER SERVED AS A MEDIATOR BETWEEN EGYPTIAN PRESIDENT, ANWAR EL SADAT AND ISRAELI PRIME MINISTER, MENACHEM BEGIN.

THESE TALKS TO EASE TENSIONS IN THE ARAB-ISRAELI CONFLICT WOULD SERVE AS A BASIS FOR CARTER'S POST-PRESIDENCY WORK.

THE FRAMEWORK WHICH CARTER HELPED TO SHAPE AT CAMP DAVID WOULD EARN THE NOBEL PEACE PRIZE FOR SADAT AND BEGIN, JOINTLY.

ALTHOUGH THE CAMP DAVID ACCORDS WERE NOT UNIVERSALLY WELL RECEIVED BY EGYPTIANS OR ISRAELIS, THE FRAMEWORKS FOR PEACE WERE A MONUMENTAL STEP TOWARD LESSENING VIOLENCE IN THE REGION.

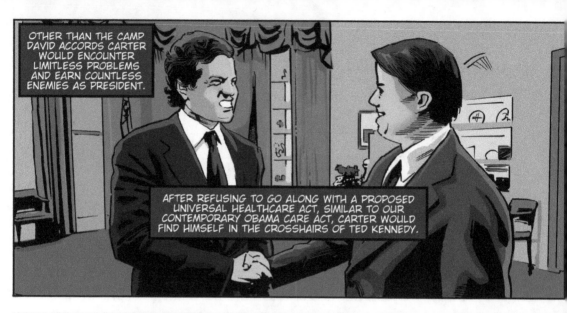

OTHER THAN THE CAMP DAVID ACCORDS CARTER WOULD ENCOUNTER LIMITLESS PROBLEMS AND EARN COUNTLESS ENEMIES AS PRESIDENT.

AFTER REFUSING TO GO ALONG WITH A PROPOSED UNIVERSAL HEALTHCARE ACT, SIMILAR TO OUR CONTEMPORARY OBAMA CARE ACT, CARTER WOULD FIND HIMSELF IN THE CROSSHAIRS OF TED KENNEDY.

THE PRESIDENT'S TREATY TO RETURN CONTROL OF THE PANAMA CANAL TO THE PANAMANIAN GOVERNMENT BROUGHT CRITICISM AND ANGER FROM POLITICIANS AND CITIZENS ALIKE.

JILL SCHUKER, WHO WAS THE DEPARTMENT OF STATE'S DEPUTY SPOKESPERSON AT THE TIME, HAD PROPOSED THAT THE PUBLIC BELIEVED THE U.S. TO BE "GIVING UP WHAT IS RIGHTFULLY OURS".

CARTER'S GREATEST CHALLENGE, AND HIS ULTIMATE DOWNFALL AS PRESIDENT, WOULD BE FORESHADOWED BY THE RISE OF A RADICAL ISLAMIC CLERIC IN IRAN.

AN UPRISING OF ISLAMIC RADICALS, UNDER THE LEADERSHIP OF AYATOLLAH KHOMEINI, HAD OUSTED IRAN'S LAWFUL RULER — SHAH MOHAMMAD REZA PAHLAVI.

THE EXILED SHAH, WHO REQUIRED SURGERY FOR GALLSTONES, WAS ALLOWED BY CARTER TO ENTER THE U.S. FOR MEDICAL TREATMENT.

CARTER'S GESTURE OF FRIENDSHIP TOWARD THE WESTERN BACKED SHAH SENT TREMORS OF ANGER THROUGH IRAN.

WITH RELIGIOUS ZEAL, KHOMEINI'S FORCES STRUCK OUT AGAINST THE UNITED STATES BY RAIDING HER EMBASSY IN TEHRAN.

52 AMERICANS FROM THE EMBASSY WOULD BE HELD HOSTAGE FOR THE NEXT 444 DAYS.

THE TRAGEDY WOULD DEFINE CARTER'S PRESIDENCY AND GREATLY WEAKEN HIS CHANCES AT A SECOND TERM.

SIX AMERICANS, WHO HAD AVOIDED CAPTURE, MANAGED TO FIND SANCTUARY IN THE EMBASSY OF THEIR NORTH AMERICAN NEIGHBORS.

WITH THE POLITICAL SITUATION BEING INCREDIBLY VOLATILE, THESE SIX AMERICANS HAD TO BE EXTRACTED IN SECRET.

THE CANADIAN GOVERNMENT, ALONG WITH PRESIDENT CARTER AND THE CIA HATCHED A PLAN TO BRING THE SIX HOME. IT WOULD GO DOWN IN HISTORY AS THE CANADIAN CAPER.

A FAKE SCIENCE FICTION FILM, ENTITLED ARGO, WAS DEVISED AS THE CRUX OF A PLOT TO EXTRACT THE AMERICANS WITHOUT ALERTING IRAN.

COMIC BOOK LEGEND, JACK KIRBY WAS EVEN HIRED TO PROVIDE BELIEVABLE CONCEPT ART FOR THE FAUX FILM.

THE OPERATION TO BRING THE SIX HOME WAS A SUCCESS. FAITH IN CARTER'S LEADERSHIP ROSE, BUT NOT FOR LONG.

OPERATION EAGLE CLAW, A BOTCHED ATTEMPT TO RESCUE THE HOSTAGES STILL HELD IN IRAN, MET WITH DISASTER.

NOT ONLY DID THE OPERATION FAIL, BUT IT COST THE LIVES OF SEVERAL AMERICAN SERVICEMEN.

CARTER HAD STATED EARLIER THAT IF TED KENNEDY RAN AGAINST HIM IN THE 1980 PRIMARIES HE WOULD "WHIP HIS ASS".

WITH ALL THE PROBLEMS HE WAS FACING THOUGH, PARTICULARLY WITH IRAN, KENNEDY'S CHALLENGE WAS NOW A TANGIBLE THREAT.

ALTHOUGH CARTER HAD MANAGED TO DEFEAT KENNEDY AFTER A BITTER PRIMARY BATTLE, HIS NEXT CHALLENGE PITTED HIM AGAINST THE FACE OF A VIBRANT AND RISING POLITICAL MOVEMENT.

CARTER, THE TROUBLED LEADER OF A DYSFUNCTIONAL PARTY, NOW HAD TO BATTLE AGAINST A REPUBLICAN JUGGERNAUT WITH A HOLLYWOOD SMILE— RONALD REAGAN.

LIKE SO MANY OTHER CHALLENGES THAT CAME CARTER'S WAY IN THOSE YEARS, THE PRESIDENT SIMPLY WAS NOT UP TO THE TASK OF DEFEATING THE INSPIRING, FORMER MOVIE STAR.

AMERICA NEEDED A HERO, AND A HERO REAGAN HAD BEEN... AT LEAST ON CELLULOID.

TO ADD INSULT TO INJURY, THE GREATEST TRAGEDY OF CARTER'S TERM EVAPORATED WITHIN MOMENTS OF REAGAN SUCCEEDING HIM.

DISHEARTENED WITH PARTY POLITICS AND WITH WASHINGTON, JIMMY AND ROSALYNN RETURNED HOME TO GEORGIA TO PLAN OUT THE NEXT PHASE OF THEIR LIVES.

AT ONLY 56 YEARS OF AGE, CARTER KNEW HE HAD A LOT MORE LIFE WITHIN HIM. HE PLANNED TO USE THAT TIME IN THE SERVICE OF SOMETHING IMPORTANT.

WHILE MOST PRESIDENTS CREATE A LIBRARY TO HOUSE THE DOCUMENTS AND ARTIFACTS WHICH CAME TO DEFINE THEIR TIME IN OFFICE, CARTER HAD GRANDER IDEAS.

THE CARTER CENTER WOULD SERVE AS A PRESIDENTIAL LIBRARY, BUT MORE IMPORTANTLY A HEADQUARTERS FOR HUMAN RIGHTS ENDEAVORS AND INDEPENDENT DIPLOMACY EFFORTS THROUGHOUT THE WORLD.

NORIEGA IS ROBBING YOU, THE PANAMANIAN PEOPLE, OF YOUR LEGITIMATE RIGHTS!

THROUGH THE CARTER CENTER, THE FORMER PRESIDENT WOULD ADDRESS TOPICS CLOSE TO HIS HEART, SUCH AS VOTER FRAUD AND HUMAN RIGHTS.

TIED IN WITH THE INTERESTS OF THE CENTER, CARTER WOULD WORK CLOSELY WITH HABITAT FOR HUMANITY, A PROGRAM TO PROVIDE HOMES FOR THOSE IN NEED.

FREE FROM PARTY TIES AND THE GILDED SHACKLES OF THE PRESIDENCY, CARTER COULD ONCE AGAIN PLAY BY HIS OWN RULES.

SOME TIMES THIS MEANT WORKING HAND IN HAND WITH CONSERVATIVES.

WE'VE REACHED AN AGREEMENT WITH NORTH KOREA, WHICH I HOPE WILL AVOID SANCTIONS.

OTHER TIMES IT WOULD MEAN WORKING AROUND DEMOCRATS.

GET ME JIMMY CARTER ON THE PHONE... NOW!

WHILE SOME STILL ARGUE THAT JIMMY CARTER'S PRESIDENCY WAS A FAILURE, IT IS INDISPUTABLE THAT HE HAS HAD ONE OF THE MOST MEANINGFUL POST-PRESIDENCIES IN AMERICAN HISTORY.

THROUGH THE CARTER CENTER HE HAS BROUGHT ENEMIES TOGETHER TO FIND COMMON GROUND, HELPED TO UPROOT DICTATORS AND POTENTIALLY DERAILED WARS. UNSURPRISINGLY, CARTER HAS EVEN EARNED THE NOBEL PEACE PRIZE.

LIKE ALL OF CARTER'S SUCCESSES IN LIFE, IT WOULD SEEM THAT THE DIPLOMATIC AND HUMANITARIAN VICTORIES HE HAS ENJOYED HAVE ALL BEEN WON ON HIS OWN TERMS.

WHEN HIS PRESIDENCY COLLAPSED, THE MAVERICK WAS REBORN. IT IS HARD TO SAY IF ANY COMMANDER-IN-CHIEF HAS EVER OUTSHINED THE POST-PRESIDENCY ACHIEVEMENTS OF THIS POLITICAL OUTSIDER.

CARTER, BEING THE TYPE TO SPEAK HIS MIND AND PLAY BY HIS OWN RULES, WAS OF COURSE BOUND TO ANGER SOME PEOPLE ALONG THE WAY.

HIS LIKENING OF THE CONFLICTS BETWEEN ISRAEL AND PALESTINE TO THE PRACTICE OF APARTHEID ENRAGED MANY JEWISH ORGANIZATIONS.

YOU ARE THE WORST EVER!

WELL AIN'T THAT THE POT CALLING THE KETTLE BLACK?

HIS COMMENTS, CONDEMNING GEORGE W. BUSH AS THE WORST PRESIDENT EVER IN TERMS OF FOREIGN POLICY, WERE MET WITH LOUD CRITICISM FROM THE RIGHTWING.

THERE WERE EVEN MEN IN WASHINGTON, OF OPPOSING POLITICAL DISPOSITIONS, WHO WOULD AGREE THAT CARTER WAS A LOOSE CANNON WHO SHOULD GO BACK TO FARMING PEANUTS.

THE CARTER CENTER

THAT BEING SAID, NO AMOUNT OF CRITICISM OR RESISTANCE HAD EVER BEEN ABLE TO DETER THIS DRIVEN MAN FROM WAGING PEACE.

AND WHAT OF THE FORMER PRESIDENT WHEN HE IS NOT TRYING TO SAVE THE WORLD?

HE IS QUITE FOND OF SHARING HIS FAITH WITH OTHERS AND STUDYING THE BIBLE.

CARTER IS ALSO AN ACCOMPLISHED AUTHOR, HAVING WRITTEN BOOKS OF NUMEROUS SUBJECTS INCLUDING MEMOIRS, POLITICAL INSIGHTS AND RELIGIOUS ANECDOTES.

PERHAPS MOST IMPORTANTLY, THE FORMER PRESIDENT CONTINUES HIS LOVE AFFAIR AND FRIENDSHIP WITH HIS DEAR WIFE ROSALYNN.

THIS MAN, WHO WAS BORN FROM THE SOIL THAT FEEDS AMERICA...

WHO SERVED HIS COUNTRY IN BODY AND MIND...

WHO LED AMERICA THROUGH INCREDIBLY UNSURE AND TUMULTUOUS TIMES...

LET US LOOK BEYOND THE MOST TROUBLING FOUR YEARS OF HIS LIFE...

AND CELEBRATE AN AMAZING LIFE SPENT IN SERVICE TO ALL MANKIND.

EPILOGUE - OCTOBER 1, 2020, PLAINS, GEORGIA.

AT 96, JIMMY CARTER IS THE LONGEST-LIVED OF HIS 44 PREDECESSORS. THE MILESTONE WAS CELEBRATED IN PLAINS WITH A PARADE.

DAY 2 OF THE 2020 DEMOCRATIC NATIONAL CONVENTION - AUGUST 18, 2020.

ALTHOUGH CAREFUL TO STAY NEUTRAL DURING THE 2020 PRESIDENTIAL PRIMARIES, JIMMY HAD THIS TO SAY:

"JOE BIDEN WAS MY FIRST AND MOST EFFECTIVE SUPPORTER IN THE SENATE. FOR DECADES, HE'S BEEN MY LOYAL AND DEDICATED FRIEND."

DEMOCRATIC NATIONAL CONVENTION

A YEAR EARLIER, JIMMY WAS ASKED IF HE'D EVER CONSIDERED RUNNING AGAIN. HE LAUGHED AT THE THOUGHT AND SAID:

"I HOPE THERE'S AN AGE LIMIT. IF I WERE JUST 80 YEARS OLD, IF I WAS 15 YEARS YOUNGER, I DON'T BELIEVE I COULD UNDERTAKE THE DUTIES I EXPERIENCED WHEN I WAS PRESIDENT."

JOE BIDEN, 77, IS NOW THE OLDEST SITTING PRESIDENT IN HISTORY. WHEN HIS TERM ENDS, HE'LL BE ALMOST 82.

AGE HASN'T SLOWED JIMMY DOWN.

IN 2015, HE UNDERWENT RADIATION TREATMENT FOR MELANOMA SPOTS ON HIS BRAIN.

HE TOLD REPORTERS, "I'LL BE PREPARED FOR ANYTHING THAT COMES."

IN 2019, HE HAD SURGERY TO REMOVE PRESSURE ON HIS BRAIN CAUSED BY A SERIES OF FALLS THAT FRACTURED HIS PELVIS AND GAVE HIM STITCHES ABOVE HIS BROW.

THE COUNTRY HELD ITS COLLECTIVE BREATH DURING THE PRESS CONFERENCE THAT FOLLOWED.

THERE ARE NO COMPLICATIONS FROM THE SURGERY. PRESIDENT AND MS. CARTER THANK EVERYONE FOR THE MANY WELL-WISHES THEY HAVE RECEIVED.

JIMMY'S NEUTRALITY DIDN'T EXTEND TO THE DISCUSSION ON VOTER RIGHTS, A HOT-BUTTON ISSUE IN GEORGIA DURING AND AFTER THE 2020 RACE. ON MARCH 9, 2021, HE SAID:

"NOW, AS OUR STATE LEGISLATORS SEEK TO TURN BACK THE CLOCK THROUGH LEGISLATION THAT WILL RESTRICT ACCESS TO VOTING FOR MANY GEORGIANS, I AM DISHEARTENED, SADDENED, AND ANGRY.

"MANY OF THE PROPOSED CHANGES ARE REACTIONS TO ALLEGATIONS OF FRAUD FOR WHICH NO EVIDENCE WAS PRODUCED. THE PROPOSED CHANGES APPEAR TO BE ROOTED IN PARTISAN INTERESTS, NOT IN THE INTERESTS OF ALL GEORGIA VOTERS."

PERHAPS THAT'S WHY HE'S ADMIRED BY SO MANY. MOST PRESIDENTS SHUN THE PUBLIC EYE AFTER A STRESSFUL FOUR OR EIGHT-YEAR STINT.

BUT JIMMY?

HE STILL HOPES FOR THE BEST FOR ALL OF US. HE ROLLS UP HIS SLEEVES, PICKS UP A HAMMER, AND GETS THE JOB DONE.

TIDALWAVE
COMICS

Curtis Lawson and Michael L. Frizell — Writer

Martin Gimenez — Art

Benjamin Glibert — Letters

Fernando Martinena — Colors

Dave Ryan — Cover

Darren G. Davis
Publisher

Maggie Jessup
Publicity

Susan Ferris
Entertainment Manager

Steven Diggs Jr.
Marketing Manager

CPSIA information can be obtained
at www.ICGtesting.com
Printed in the USA
LVHW051207290921
699024LV00003B/230

9 781955 712569

OKAY, THEN TELL ME THE STORY AGAIN, PAPA.

THE STORY OF GREGORIO CORTEZ? AND ABOUT TEJANO AND CONJUNTO MUSIC?

YES, PLEASE! TELL IT!

WELL, GREGORIO WAS BORN ON A RANCH IN 1875...

NO! SING IT, TOO!

PATIENCE, SELENA. I HAVE TO SET THE STORY UP.

'KAY. HURRY!

MOVING FROM PLACE TO PLACE AS A RANCH HAND WAS A HARD LIFE, BUT HE FINALLY SETTLED IN KARNES COUNTY, TEXAS, IN 1900.

ON JUNE 12, 1901, SHERIFF MORRIS VISITED THE CORTEZ RESIDENCE LOOKING FOR A HORSE THIEF...

<THERE YOU GO. EAT UP.>*

*TRANSLATED FROM SPANISH.

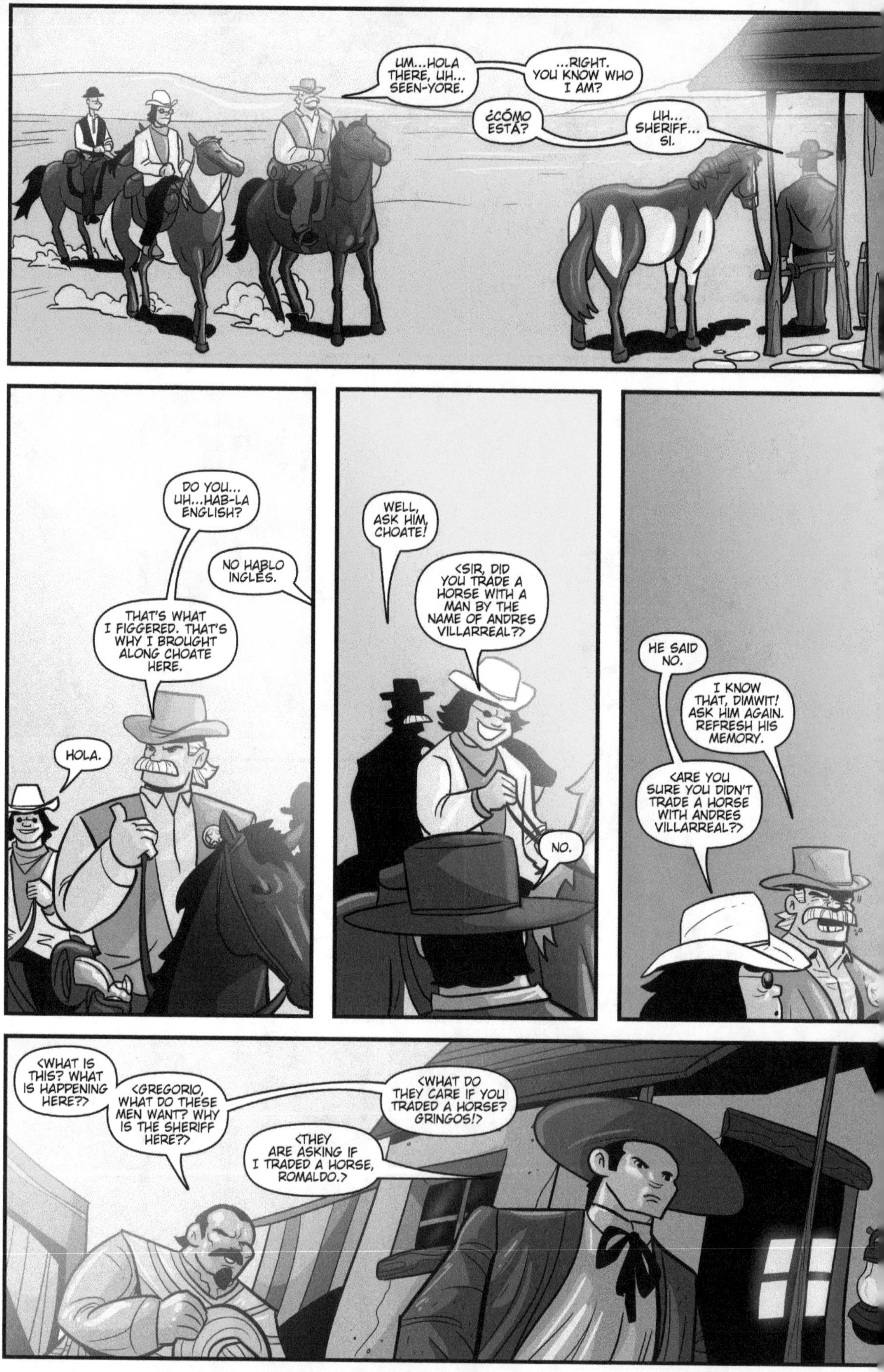
UM...HOLA THERE, UH... SEEN-YORE.
¿CÓMO ESTÁ?
...RIGHT. YOU KNOW WHO I AM?
UH... SHERIFF... SI.
DO YOU... UH...HAB-LA ENGLISH?
NO HABLO INGLÉS.
THAT'S WHAT I FIGGERED. THAT'S WHY I BROUGHT ALONG CHOATE HERE.
HOLA.
WELL, ASK HIM, CHOATE!
<SIR, DID YOU TRADE A HORSE WITH A MAN BY THE NAME OF ANDRES VILLARREAL?>
NO.
HE SAID NO.
I KNOW THAT, DIMWIT! ASK HIM AGAIN. REFRESH HIS MEMORY.
<ARE YOU SURE YOU DIDN'T TRADE A HORSE WITH ANDRES VILLARREAL?>
<WHAT IS THIS? WHAT IS HAPPENING HERE?>
<GREGORIO, WHAT DO THESE MEN WANT? WHY IS THE SHERIFF HERE?>
<THEY ARE ASKING IF I TRADED A HORSE, ROMALDO.>
<WHAT DO THEY CARE IF YOU TRADED A HORSE? GRINGOS!>

WHAT'S ALL THAT ABOUT?

I... THEY'RE TALKING TOO FAST... I CAN'T...

I THOUGHT YOU WERE SOME KINDA MEXICAN EXPERT?

JUST FIND OUT WHETHER THEY TRADED FOR THE DAMN HORSE OR NOT!

TELL THEM IF THEY DON'T TELL ME, I'M GOING TO ARREST THEM.

<YOU WILL BE ARRESTED IF YOU DON'T TELL US ABOUT TRADING THE HORSE!>

<I TRADED NO HORSE! I TRADED A MARE!>

WAIT!... <I...I DO NOT UNDERSTAND YOU. SLOW DOWN!>

<YOU PEOPLE ARE ALWAYS HARASSING US! GREGORIO'S DONE NOTHING WRONG! HE TRADED A MARE, NOT A HORSE!>

<STAY CALM!>

HE'S REACHING!

KRRCHIK

BLAM

UGHNN

<BROTHER!>

KRATACK-KA-BLAM

AHHH...

SHERIFF! DAMN MEXICANS!

NO! STOP! STOP!

TRIMMEL! MORRIS IS HURT! C'MON! C'MON!

BLAM BLAM

♫♫ EN EL CONDADO DEL CARMEN MIREN LO QUE HA SUCEDIDO: MURIÓ EL CHERIFE MAYOR, QUEDANDO ROMÁN HERIDO. ♫♫

♫♫ LOOK WHAT HAS HAPPENED IN THE COUNTY OF CARMEN: THE MAJOR SHERIFF HAS DIED AND ROMÁN HAS BEEN WOUNDED. ♫♫

UHN... <THEY...THEY ARE GONE?>

♫♫ OTRO DÍA POR LA MAÑANA CUANDO LA GENTE LLEGÓ, UNOS A LOS OTROS DICEN: "NO SABEN QUIEN LO MATÓ". ♫♫

♫♫ THE NEXT MORNING, WHEN PEOPLE ARRIVED, THEY SAID TO EACH OTHER: "NOBODY KNOWS WHO KILLED HIM." ♫♫

♫♫ SE ANDUVIERON INFORMANDO, COMO TRES HORAS DESPUÉS SUPIERON QUE EL MALHECHOR ERA GREGORIO CORTEZ. ♫♫

♫♫ THEY INVESTIGATED AND ABOUT THREE HOURS LATER THEY DISCOVERED THAT GREGORIO CORTEZ WAS THE WRONGDOER. ♫♫

OH! 3000 PESOS! IS THAT ENOUGH TO BUY NEW BOOTS?

WANTED
— ● DEAD OR ALIVE ● —

Gregorio Cortez

For **Murder**

Reward:
3000 pesos

HA! PERHAPS.

♫♫ DECÍA GREGORIO CORTEZ CON SU ALMA MUY ENCENDIDA: "NO SIENTO HABERLO MATADO, LA DEFENSA ES PERMITIDA". ♫♫

♫♫ GREGORIO CORTEZ SAID, WITH HIS SOUL ABLAZE: "I'M NOT SORRY FOR KILLING HIM, SELF-DEFENSE IS JUSTIFIABLE. ♫♫

♫♫ VENÍAN LOS AMERICANOS QUE POR EL VIENTO VOLABAN PORQUE SE IBAN A GANAR TRES MIL PESOS QUE LES DABAN. ♫♫

♫♫ THE AMERICANS WERE COMING AS FAST AS THE WIND, BECAUSE THEY WOULD EARN A REWARD OF 3,000 PESOS. ♫♫

♫♫ TIRÓ CON RUMBO A GONZÁLEZ, VARIOS CHERIFES LO VIERON, NO LO QUISIERON SEGUIR PORQUE LE TUVIERON MIEDO. ♫♫

♫♫ HE FLED TOWARD GONZÁLEZ. SEVERAL SHERIFFS SAW HIM BUT THEY DIDN'T WANT TO PURSUE HIM BECAUSE THEY WERE AFRAID. ♫♫

WHAT SHALL WE DO IF WE FIND HIM? IN AN OPEN CONFRONTATION, ONLY A FEW OF US WILL MAKE IT BACK.

LOOK!

CALL THE MEN!

GUAU GUAU GRRR-ROWL

♫♫ EN EL REDONDEL DEL RANCHO LO ALCANZARON A RODEAR, POQUITOS MÁS DE TRESCIENTOS Y ALLÍ LES BRINCÓ EL CORRAL. ♫♫

♫♫ BY THE CORRAL OF THE RANCH THEY SURROUNDED HIM. THERE WERE MORE THAN 300 MEN, BUT HE JUMPED THROUGH THEIR RING. ♫♫

♫♫ ALLÁ POR EL ENCINAL, ASEGÚN POR LO QUE DICEN, SE AGARRARON A BALAZOS Y LES MATÓ A OTRO CHERIFE. ♫♫

♫♫ AROUND EL ENCINAL, ACCORDING TO WHAT THEY SAY, THEY HAD A SHOOT-OUT AND HE KILLED ANOTHER SHERIFF. ♫♫

♫♫ DECÍA GREGORIO CORTEZ CON SU PISTOLA EN LA MANO: ♫♫

♫♫ GREGORIO CORTEZ SAID, WITH HIS PISTOL IN HIS HAND: "DON'T RUN YOU COWARDLY RANGERS, FROM ONE LONE MEXICAN.

"NO CORRAN RINCHES COBARDES, CON UN SOLO MEXICANO".

♫♫ GIRÓ CON RUMBO A LAREDO SIN NINGUNA TIMIDEZ: ♫♫

"¡SÍGANME RINCHES COBARDES, YO SOY GREGORIO CORTEZ!"

♫♫ HE TURNED TOWARD LAREDO WITHOUT ANY FEAR: "FOLLOW ME, YOU COWARDLY RANGERS, I AM GREGORIO CORTEZ." ♫♫

OH! I KNOW WHAT HAPPENS NEXT!

BE CALM, PRECIOSA!

BUT I KNOW WHAT HAPPENS, PAPA! THEY CAN'T CATCH HIM...HE HAS TO TURN HIMSELF IN BECAUSE HE'S SO FAST!

1976: CORPUS CHRISTI, TEXAS

IS THAT ALL YOU LEARNED? THAT CORTEZ WAS SOME KIND OF SUPERHERO?

ABRAHAM QUNITANILLA JR.! ARE YOU TELLING THAT TERRIBLE FOLKTALE AGAIN?

IT'S NOT TERRIBLE, MAMA. STORIES LIKE THAT ARE WHY WE HAVE TEJANO AND CONJUNTO MUSIC! I LOVE TEJANO!

SHE LOVES TEJANO! AND YOU SING IT SO WELL, PRECIOSA. BUT WHAT DID THE STORY TELL YOU?

THAT I SHOULD ALSO LEARN TO SPEAK SPANISH. BUT IT'S SO HARD!

BUT YOU SING IN SPANISH!

I BARELY KNOW WHAT I'M SAYING! I JUST LIKE THE SOUND OF IT WHEN I SING!

MY SILLY LITTLE SEL.

SO...WHAT KIND OF MUSIC HAS INFLUENCED TEJANO?

IT'S COUNTRY MUSIC, IT'S JAZZ, IT HAS ROOTS OF GERMAN POLKA, IT ALSO HAS MEXICAN MUSIC IN IT. I LIKE THE ACCORDION.

...

WHY THAT LOOK, PRECIOSA?

GRANDMA AND GRANDPA WERE FROM MEXICO. SO THAT MAKES YOU MEXICAN. MAMA IS HALF-MEXICAN AND HALF CHEROKEE INDIAN.

YES?

SO WHAT DOES THAT MAKE ME?

AMERICAN.

BUT THERE IS ANOTHER LESSON TO BE LEARNED HERE, SELENA.

WHAT LESSON, PAPA?

THAT GREAT THINGS COME FROM HUMBLE BEGINNINGS. THAT YOU MUST FIGHT FOR, AND DEFEND, WHAT YOU KNOW TO BE RIGHT IN YOUR HEART.

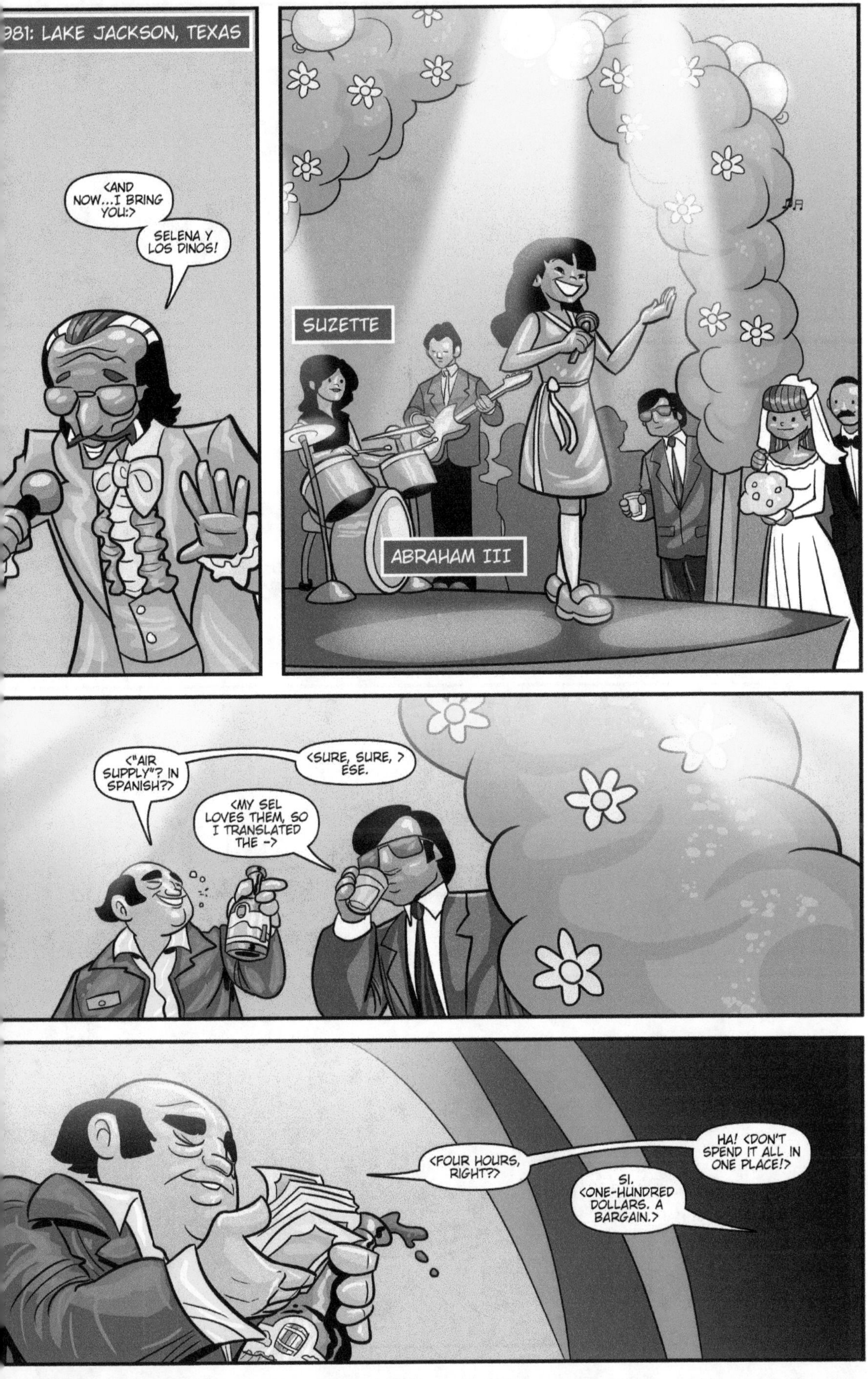
981: LAKE JACKSON, TEXAS
<AND NOW...I BRING YOU:>
SELENA Y LOS DINOS!
SUZETTE
ABRAHAM III
<"AIR SUPPLY"? IN SPANISH?>
<MY SEL LOVES THEM, SO I TRANSLATED THE ->
<SURE, SURE, > ESE.
<FOUR HOURS, RIGHT?>
SI. <ONE-HUNDRED DOLLARS. A BARGAIN.>
HA! <DON'T SPEND IT ALL IN ONE PLACE!>

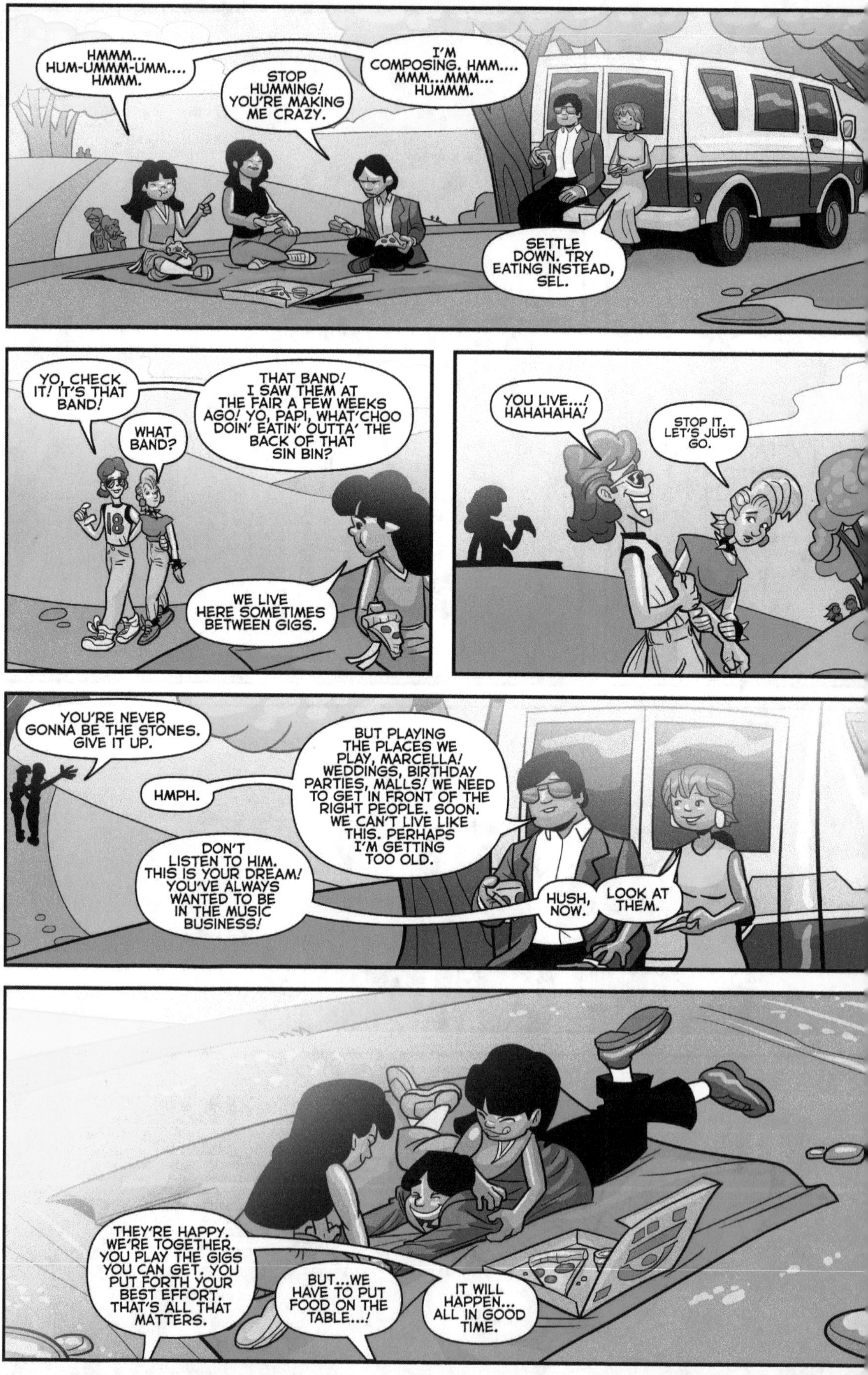

HMMM... HUM-UMMM-UMM.... HMMM.
STOP HUMMING! YOU'RE MAKING ME CRAZY.
I'M COMPOSING. HMM.... MMM...MMM... HUMMM.
SETTLE DOWN. TRY EATING INSTEAD, SEL.
YO, CHECK IT! IT'S THAT BAND!
WHAT BAND?
THAT BAND! I SAW THEM AT THE FAIR A FEW WEEKS AGO! YO, PAPI, WHAT'CHOO DOIN' EATIN' OUTTA' THE BACK OF THAT SIN BIN?
WE LIVE HERE SOMETIMES BETWEEN GIGS.
YOU LIVE...! HAHAHAHA!
STOP IT. LET'S JUST GO.
YOU'RE NEVER GONNA BE THE STONES. GIVE IT UP.
HMPH.
BUT PLAYING THE PLACES WE PLAY, MARCELLA! WEDDINGS, BIRTHDAY PARTIES, MALLS! WE NEED TO GET IN FRONT OF THE RIGHT PEOPLE. SOON. WE CAN'T LIVE LIKE THIS. PERHAPS I'M GETTING TOO OLD.
DON'T LISTEN TO HIM. THIS IS YOUR DREAM! YOU'VE ALWAYS WANTED TO BE IN THE MUSIC BUSINESS!
HUSH, NOW.
LOOK AT THEM.
THEY'RE HAPPY. WE'RE TOGETHER. YOU PLAY THE GIGS YOU CAN GET. YOU PUT FORTH YOUR BEST EFFORT. THAT'S ALL THAT MATTERS.
BUT...WE HAVE TO PUT FOOD ON THE TABLE...!
IT WILL HAPPEN... ALL IN GOOD TIME.

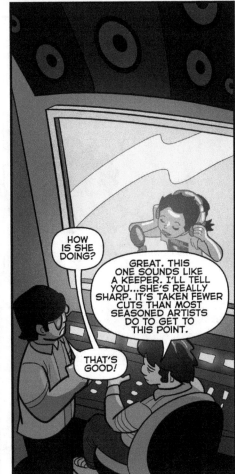

HOW IS SHE DOING?

GREAT. THIS ONE SOUNDS LIKE A KEEPER. I'LL TELL YOU...SHE'S REALLY SHARP. IT'S TAKEN FEWER CUTS THAN MOST SEASONED ARTISTS DO TO GET TO THIS POINT.

THAT'S GOOD!

STILL...

WHAT IS IT?

SHE'S SO... YOUNG. SO RAW.

THAT'S PART OF HER APPEAL.

WELL, I WAS TALKING WITH THE PRODUCER. WE THINK SHE'S NEEDS MORE... SEASONING.

I DON'T AGREE!

WE'LL FINISH THIS ALBUM OF COURSE. WE'LL PROBABLY RELEASE "SE ACABO AQUEL AMOR," MAYBE "TRES VECES NO," AND DEFINITELY "YA SE VA." YOU'LL GET SOME RADIO PLAY.

1985: CARA RECORDS STUDIO, RECORDING SESSION FOR THE NEW GIRL IN TOWN

HEH. LOOK AT HER: A REGULAR MEXICAN MADONNA.

YES, YES. HOW IS SHE DOING?

WANNA HEAR FOR YOURSELF? SHE'S GOOD... STRONG. BUT...

I'VE HEARD IT. BUT WHAT?

WELL... THIS GENRE IS A MALE-DOMINATED ONE. THIS TEJANO.

- IS TALENTED, MR. QUNITANILLA, I'LL GRANT THAT. BUT THIS ALBUM...WELL...THERE'S TALK IT WON'T BE RELEASED AS A WHOLE.

I KNOW, I KNOW, BUT SELENA –

WHAT! BUT... THERE'S TEN TRACKS! TEN!

THAT'S FINE, SELENA. JUST GREAT. WE'LL GO WITH THIS ONE.

DON'T WORRY, MR. QUINTANILLA. MANNY WILL PROBABLY RELEASE THE SONGS AS 45'S. AFTER THE LAST ALBUM...

IT WAS ENOUGH TIME TO GET MANNY GUERRA'S ATTENTION.

FREDDIE RECORDS ONLY GAVE US TWO MONTHS OF PLAY! TWO MONTHS... NOT ENOUGH TIME.

BUT HE HEARD US IN CONCERT, NOT –

PAPA, HOW WAS THAT? PAPA?

WONDERFUL, PRECIOSA. JUST WONDERFUL.

"... Y GRACIAS A DIOS ESTAMOS ATASCADOS A ÉL, ¿SABES? HEMOS VENIDO DESDE MUY LEJOS. REAL Y VERDADERAMENTE.

(...AND GOODNESS THANK WE STUCK TO IT, YOU KNOW? WE'VE COME A LONG WAY. REALLY AND TRULY.)

"... NO PUEDO... ME IMAGINO QUE TODOS LOS DÍAS DE TRABAJO Y ENTRAR EN UNA OFICINA."

("I CAN'T UM...IMAGINE ME HAVE EVERYDAY JOB AND GO INTO AN OFFICE.")

"NO PUEDO IMAGINARME EN EL LUGAR MISMO TODOS LOS DÍAS."

("I CAN'T PICTURE ME GOING INTO THE PLACE SAME EVERYDAY.")

⟨THANK YOU, SELENA. IS THERE ANYTHING ELSE YOU'D LIKE TO ADD?⟩

⟨JUST I'M READY FOR NEXT STEP YOU KNOW? WATCH OUT, WORLD!⟩

⟨THANK YOU, SELENA. I'M WITH SELENA, WHO INSISTED ON BEING INTERVIEWED IN SPANISH AND WHO HAS JUST WON THE FEMALE VOCALIST OF THE YEAR, AGAIN, AT THE TEJANO MUSIC AWARDS!⟩

"SELENA, YOU KNOW I DON'T LIKE YOU DRESSING LIKE...THAT."

"LIKE WHAT, PAPA?"

"THAT! RUNNING ABOUT SHIRTLESS!"

"IT'S JUST A BRA! MY STYLE! MY SIGNATURE! PERHAPS I'LL... I'LL OPEN UP MY OWN SHOPS AND SELL THEM!"

"YOUR VOICE IS YOUR SIGNATURE, PRECIOSA."

"I JUST WANT THEM TO SEE YOU FOR WHO YOU ARE AND HEAR WHAT YOU CAN DO. NOT BLINDED BY...THOSE."

"DON'T BE SILLY, PAPA! WHAT I DO ONSTAGE, YOU WON'T CATCH ME DOING OFFSTAGE. I MEAN, I THINK DEEP DOWN I'M STILL KIND OF LIKE, TIMID AND MODEST ABOUT A LOT OF THINGS."

"COULD HAVE FOOLED ME."

"BUT ON STAGE, I RELEASE ALL THAT; I LET GO!"

NOW, I'M READY.

1988

CAN WE TRY THE REFRAIN AGAIN? I'M HAVING SOME DIFFICULTY IN THE THIRD MEASURE.

YEAH, HEARD THAT.

HA! GEE, THANKS.

KNOCK KNOCK!

I'D LIKE TO INTRODUCE YOU TO CHRIS PEREZ.

HEY.

CHRIS PLAYED WITH SHELLY LARES AND EVEN HAS HIS OWN BAND. I WANT TO HIRE HIM TO JOIN US.

CHRIS, THIS IS SUZETTE, ABRAHAM, AND OF COURSE, SELENA.

I'M CHRIS.

SELENA.

I KNOW.

I'M GLAD YOU KNOW.

OH, BROTHER.

OH SHUT UP.

"PRECIOSA! YOU CAN'T BE SERIOUS!"

"I AM, PAPA. THIS IS RIGHT. THIS IS REAL. FIRING HIM DIDN'T BREAK US UP. WE WERE FRIENDS FIRST, PAPA. I NEVER THOUGHT I'D WANT TO MARRY A MUSICIAN."

"I WILL FOLLOW WHAT MY HEART TELLS ME. AND IT TELLS ME THAT CHRIS IS THE ONE."

"THE...ONE. SEL, WHY MUST YOU ALWAYS BE SO STRONG-WILLED?"

"HMM...I WONDER WHERE I GET IT, PAPA?"

APRIL 2, 1992: NUECES COUNTY, TEXAS

"REMEMBER, SEL, TO SHARE AND TO ALWAYS TREAT PEOPLE THE WAY YOU WANT THEM TO TREAT YOU."

"IN 1988, MY SEL... AHEM...I'M SORRY."

"IT'S OKAY. I UNDERSTAND, MR. QUINTANILLA. PLEAS CONTINUE."

"...SIGNED WITH CAPITAL EMI'S LATIN LABEL IN A MOVE THAT WAS, ARGUABLY, HER BIG BREAK. SHE ALSO HAD A LUCRATIVE CONTRACT ENDORSING PEPSI PRODUCTS. A SPECIAL BOTTLE COMMEMORATING HER TIME WITH THE COMPANY WAS SOLD IN 1995. THAT'S WHERE HER MONEY CAME FROM."

"I READ THAT SHE DOMINATED THE TEJANO MUSIC AWARDS FOR TEN YEARS, WINNING BEST FEMALE VOCALIST FOR EIGHT YEARS IN A ROW."

"YES."

"AN INCREDIBLE ACHIEVEMENT."

"JUST ONE OF MANY. OH, MY PRECIOSA."

APRIL 2, 1995:
CORPUS CHRISTI, TEXAS

JUST TAKE YOUR TIME AND TELL THE STORY ANY WAY YOU LIKE.

OKAY.

WHEN DID YOUR DAUGHTER MEET YOLANDA SALD –

NO! DO NOT SAY HER NAME!

ALL RIGHT.

WE HIRED HER TO RUN SEL'S FAN CLUB. SHE TRUSTS... TRUSTED... HER.

MISS... AH... SHE ALSO WORKED AS THE...BUSINESS MANAGER FOR YOUR DAUGHTER'S CLOTHING BOUTIQUES?

YES, SELENA, ETC.

WE'D NOTICED IRREGULARITIES.

IRREGULARITIES.

IN THE BOOKS. MONEY WAS MISSING, FAN CLUB MEMBERS WERE COMPLAINING ABOUT NOT RECEIVING MERCHANDISE. SEL DIDN'T BELIEVE IT. THEY WERE FRIENDS, YOU SEE. FRIENDS.

TAKE YOUR TIME. WOULD YOU LIKE SOME COFFEE?

NO.

JUST AS WELL, STUFF'S SWILL STRAINED THROUGH AN OLD SOCK. BUT IT KEEPS ME FRISKY.

RIGHT. SURE.

OKAY. SO, YOU'D NOTICED IRREGULARITIES IN THE BOOKS.

YES. SHE'D WRITTEN FOUR CHECKS TO HERSELF FOR $3000 FROM THE FAN CLUB'S ACCOUNTS. I WAS ANGRY. I CONFRONTED HER. SHE SAID SHE COULD EXPLAIN IT ALL IF I JUST CALMED DOWN AND GAVE HER THE TIME.

WHY DID YOUR DAUGHTER GO TO THE DAYS INN?

TO MEET... HER. TO GET DOCUMENTS SHE'D STOLEN.

DOCUMENTS.

FOR TAX PURPOSES. SHE WAS COVERING HER TRACKS, BUT SEL...SHE ALWAYS SAW THE BEST IN PEOPLE. BELIEVED IN THEM.

"OF COURSE. SO, SHE GOES TO THE DAYS INN..."

"SHE STOOD UP FOR WHAT SHE BELIEVED TO BE RIGHT. SHE GREW UP WITH MORAL AND ALSO RESPECT. FOR EVERYONE. OUR FAITH, JEHOVAH'S WITNESS, REQUESTS NO LESS. PLEASE. TELL ME WHAT HAPPENED TO SELENA."

‹IT'S OKAY...HOLD ON... I'M HERE.›

‹I'M HERE.›

"SO...THEY LEFT?"

RIGHT. I USUALLY DON'T LET HER LEAVE THE HOUSE WITHOUT KNOWING WHERE SHE WAS GOING, BUT I WAS ASLEEP.

YES, BUT AS HER HUSBAND, YOU NOTICED SHE'D LEFT?

I MEAN, I HEARD HER, BUT I DIDN'T WANT TO GET UP, YOU KNOW? I THOUGHT MAYBE SHE WAS GOING TO HANG OUT WITH MY DAD WHO HAD STAYED OVER THAT NIGHT.

I DIDN'T EVEN THINK TO ASK AND THEN... SHE WAS GONE.

I'M SORRY.

WHY DID THEY LEAVE THE HOTEL? I THOUGHT YOU FOUND –

WE'RE STILL PIECING THAT TOGETHER, BUT SELENA BELIEVED THAT...HER FORMER EMPLOYEE...HAD BEEN RAPED.

I DON'T UNDERSTAND... RAPED?

SHE TOLD SELENA SHE'D BEEN RAPED AND THAT THE PAPERS SHE INTENDED TO RETURN WERE IN HER CAR, WHICH WAS STOLEN.

SHE SAID NOTHING ABOUT IT WHEN WE WERE THERE EARLIER IN THE DAY. SHE STALLED US, CLEARLY LYING. SELENA AND I LEFT. BUT...SHE CALLED THAT NIGHT. I KNOW THAT... NOW.

COFFEE?

NO, THANK YOU. I'M CONFUSED. HOW DO YOU KNOW ABOUT SOME RAPE?

SELANA TOOK HER TO A HOSPITAL. THE RAPE KIT WAS NEGATIVE, SO SELENA RETURNED TO THE DAYS INN.

AND... AND THAT'S WHEN IT HAPPENED. WHY DIDN'T SHE BRING ME?

WE... PRESUME THAT THE RAPE STORY WAS A WAY TO GET SELENA TO COME ALONE.

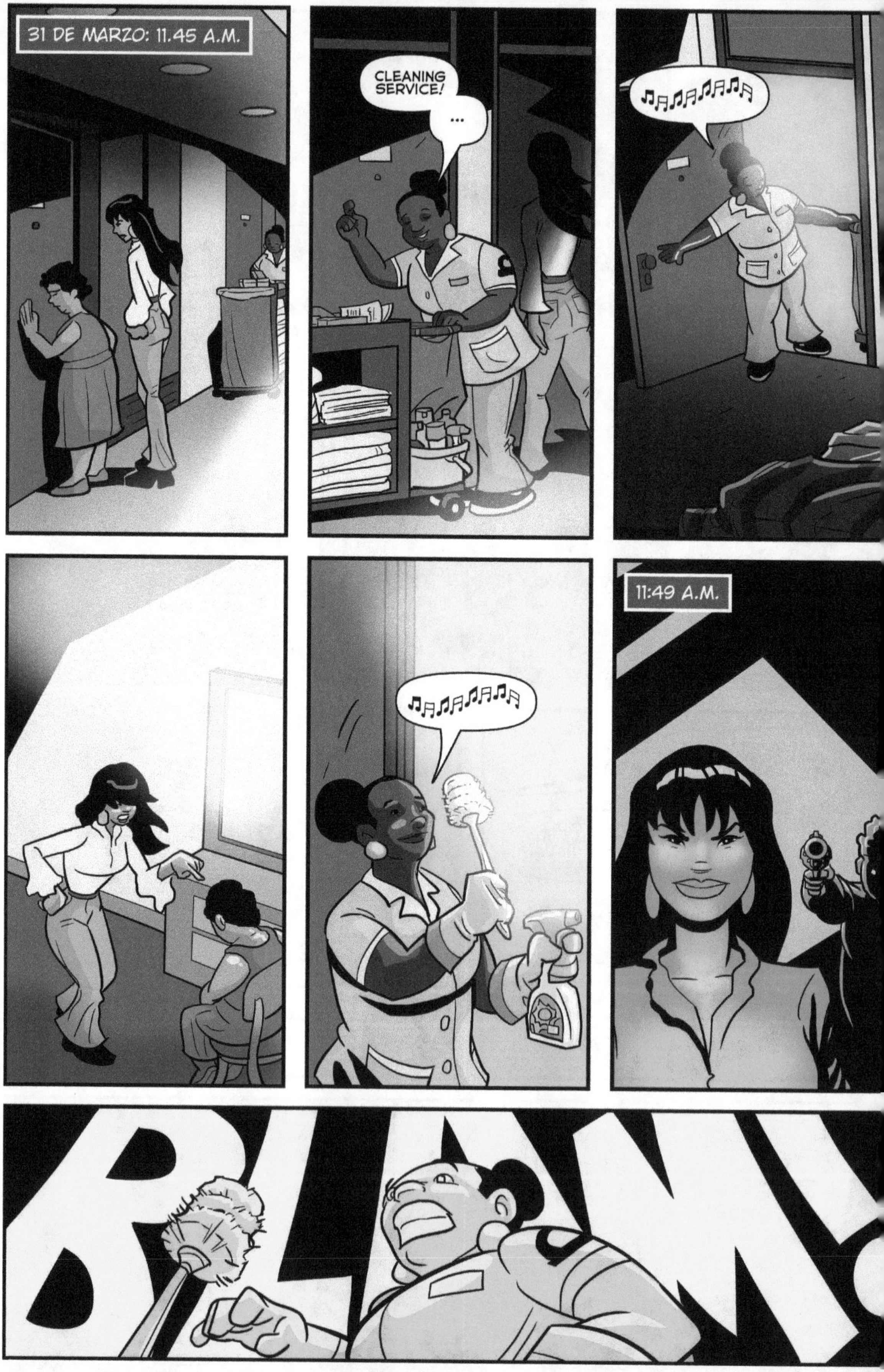
31 DE MARZO: 11.45 A.M.
CLEANING SERVICE!
...
11:49 A.M.
BLAM

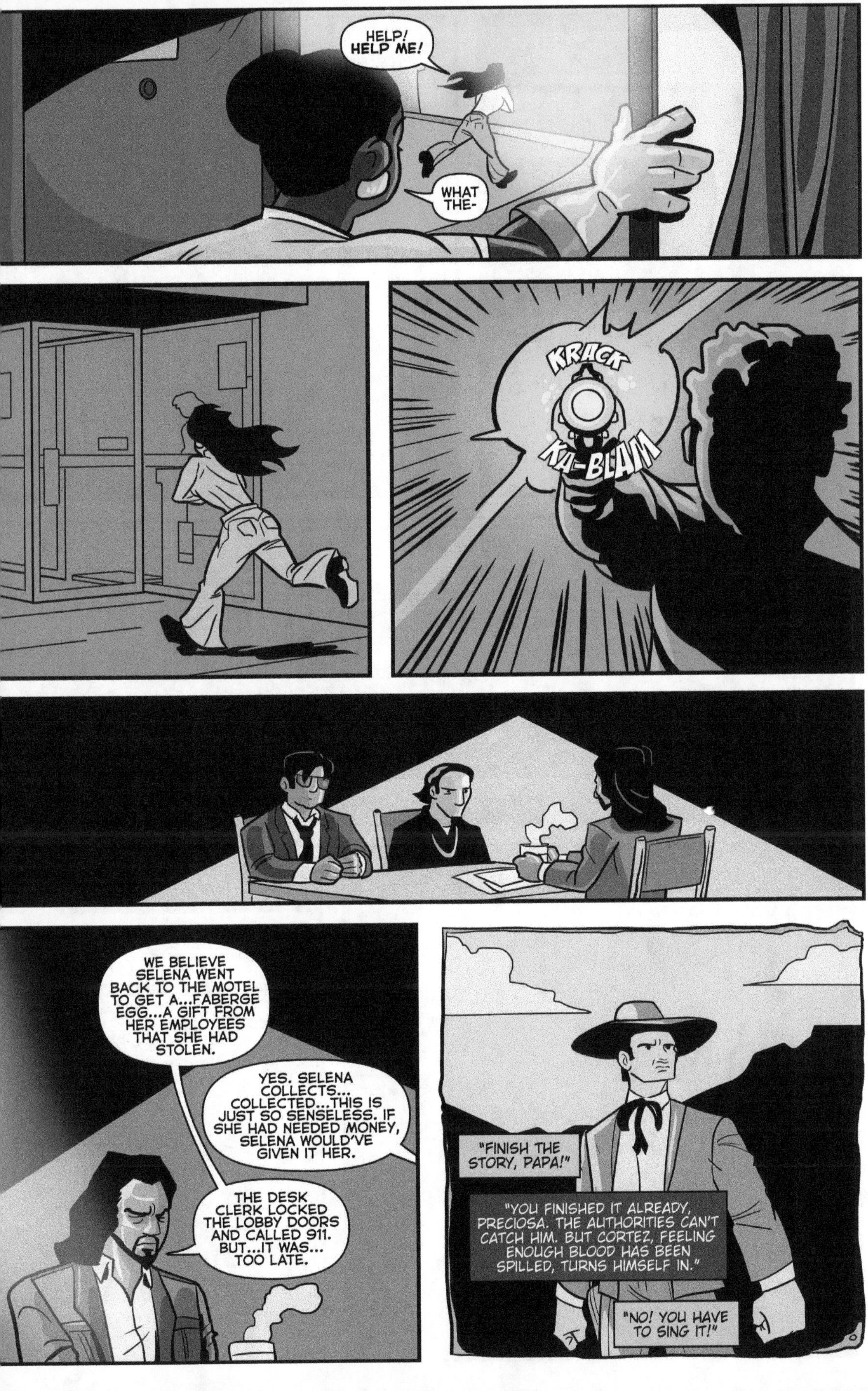
HELP! HELP ME!
WHAT THE-
KRACK
KA-BLAM
WE BELIEVE SELENA WENT BACK TO THE MOTEL TO GET A...FABERGE EGG...A GIFT FROM HER EMPLOYEES THAT SHE HAD STOLEN.
YES. SELENA COLLECTS... COLLECTED...THIS IS JUST SO SENSELESS. IF SHE HAD NEEDED MONEY, SELENA WOULD'VE GIVEN IT HER.
THE DESK CLERK LOCKED THE LOBBY DOORS AND CALLED 911. BUT...IT WAS... TOO LATE.
"FINISH THE STORY, PAPA!"
"YOU FINISHED IT ALREADY, PRECIOSA. THE AUTHORITIES CAN'T CATCH HIM. BUT CORTEZ, FEELING ENOUGH BLOOD HAS BEEN SPILLED, TURNS HIMSELF IN."
"NO! YOU HAVE TO SING IT!"

♫♫ GREGORIO LE DICE A JUAN EN EL RANCHO DEL CIPRÉS: "PLATÍCAME QUÉ HAY DE NUEVO, YO SOY GREGORIO CORTEZ". ♫♫

♫♫ GREGORIO SAYS TO JUAN, AT THE RANCH OF THE CYPRESS: "TELL ME, WHAT'S NEW? I AM GREGORIO CORTEZ." ♫♫

♫♫ GREGORIO LE DICE A JUAN: "MUY PRONTO LO VAS A VER, ANDA HÁBLALE A LOS CHERIFES QUE ME VENGAN A APREHENDER". ♫♫

♫♫ GREGORIO SAYS TO JUAN: "YOU WILL SOON FIND OUT. GO AND CALL THE SHERIFFS, TELL THEM TO COME AND ARREST ME." ♫♫

♫♫ CUANDO LLEGAN LOS CHERIFES GREGORIO SE PRESENTÓ: "POR LAS BUENAS SI ME LLEVAN, PORQUE DE OTRO MODO NO". ♫♫

♫♫ WHEN THE SHERIFFS ARRIVED GREGORIO TURNED HIMSELF IN. "YOU CAN TAKE ME ONLY ON MY TERMS, NO OTHER WAY." ♫♫

♫♫ YA AGARRARON A CORTEZ, YA TERMINÓ LA CUESTIÓN, LA POBRE DE SU FAMILIA LA LLEVA EN EL CORAZÓN. ♫♫

♫♫ THEY CAUGHT CORTEZ AND THE CASE IS CLOSED. HIS POOR FAMILY IS ALWAYS IN HIS HEART. ♫♫

SEASIDE MEMORIAL PARK: CORPUS CHRISTI, TEXAS

♫♫ YA CON ESTA AHÍ ME DESPIDO CON LA SOMBRA DE UN CIPRÉS, AQUÍ SE ACABA CANTANDO LA TRAGEDIA DE CORTEZ. ♫♫

♫♫ I NOW TAKE MY LEAVE, BY THE SHADE OF A CYPRESS TREE. HERE I END SINGING THE TRAGEDY OF CORTEZ. ♫♫

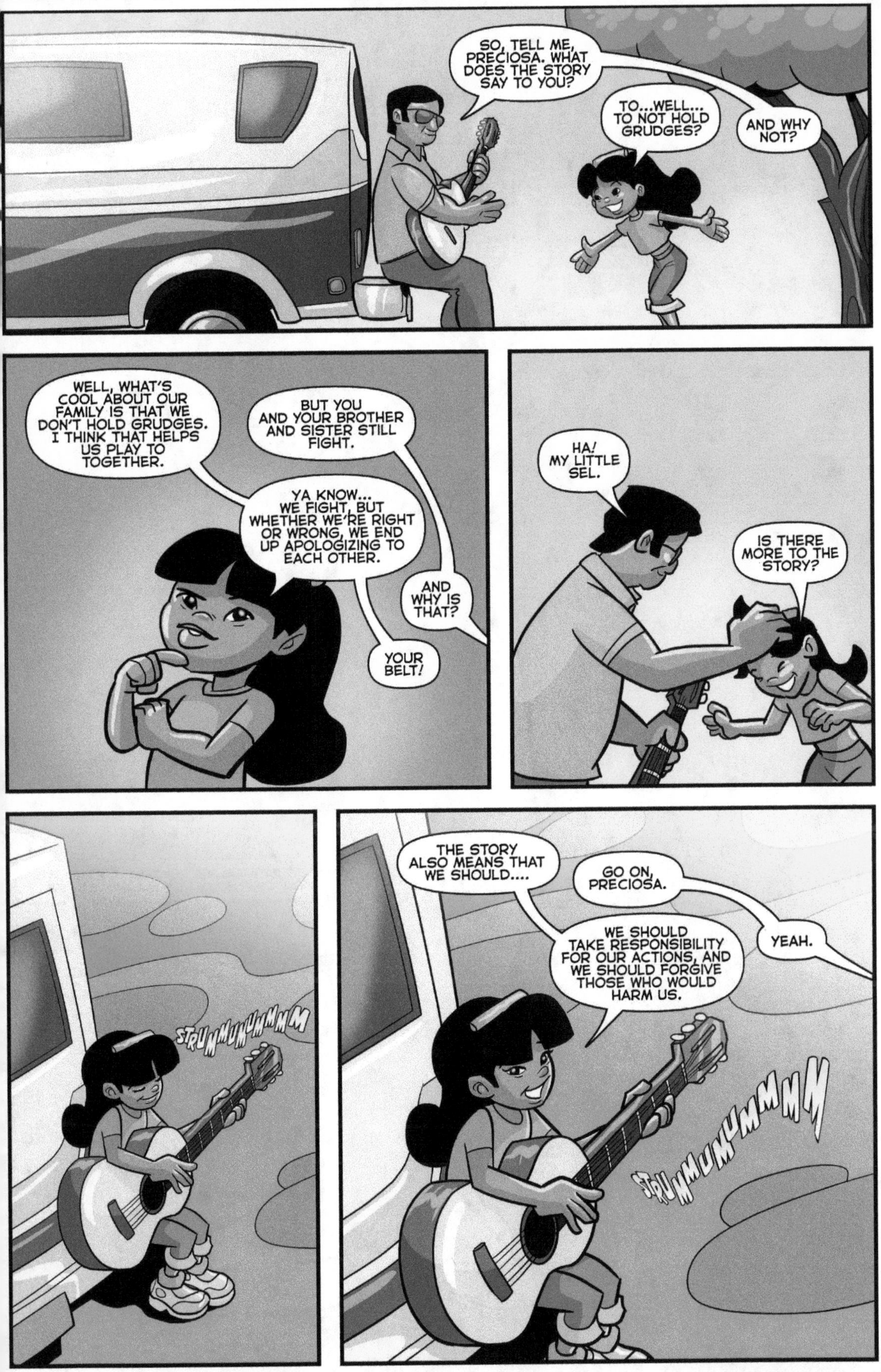
SO, TELL ME, PRECIOSA. WHAT DOES THE STORY SAY TO YOU?
TO...WELL... TO NOT HOLD GRUDGES?
AND WHY NOT?
WELL, WHAT'S COOL ABOUT OUR FAMILY IS THAT WE DON'T HOLD GRUDGES. I THINK THAT HELPS US PLAY TO TOGETHER.
BUT YOU AND YOUR BROTHER AND SISTER STILL FIGHT.
YA KNOW... WE FIGHT, BUT WHETHER WE'RE RIGHT OR WRONG, WE END UP APOLOGIZING TO EACH OTHER.
AND WHY IS THAT?
YOUR BELT!
HA! MY LITTLE SEL.
IS THERE MORE TO THE STORY?
STRUMMUMUMMMM
THE STORY ALSO MEANS THAT WE SHOULD....
GO ON, PRECIOSA.
WE SHOULD TAKE RESPONSIBILITY FOR OUR ACTIONS, AND WE SHOULD FORGIVE THOSE WHO WOULD HARM US.
YEAH.
STRUMMUMUMMMMN

TO DATE, SELENA QUINTANILLA-PEREZ HAS SOLD OVER 60 MILLION ALBUMS WORLDWIDE.

COMICS

Michael L. Frizell ————————————————○ Writer

Ramon Salas ————————————————○ Art

Benjamin Glibert ————————————————○ Letters

Darren G. Davis ————————————————○ Editor

Ramon Salas ————————————————○ Cover

Darren G. Davis
Publisher

Maggie Jessup
Publicity

Susan Ferris
Entertainment Manager

Steven Diggs Jr.
Marketing Manager

Cover B: Dave Ryan

Cover C : Joe Paradise with Pablo Martinena

Translate by: Axcalay

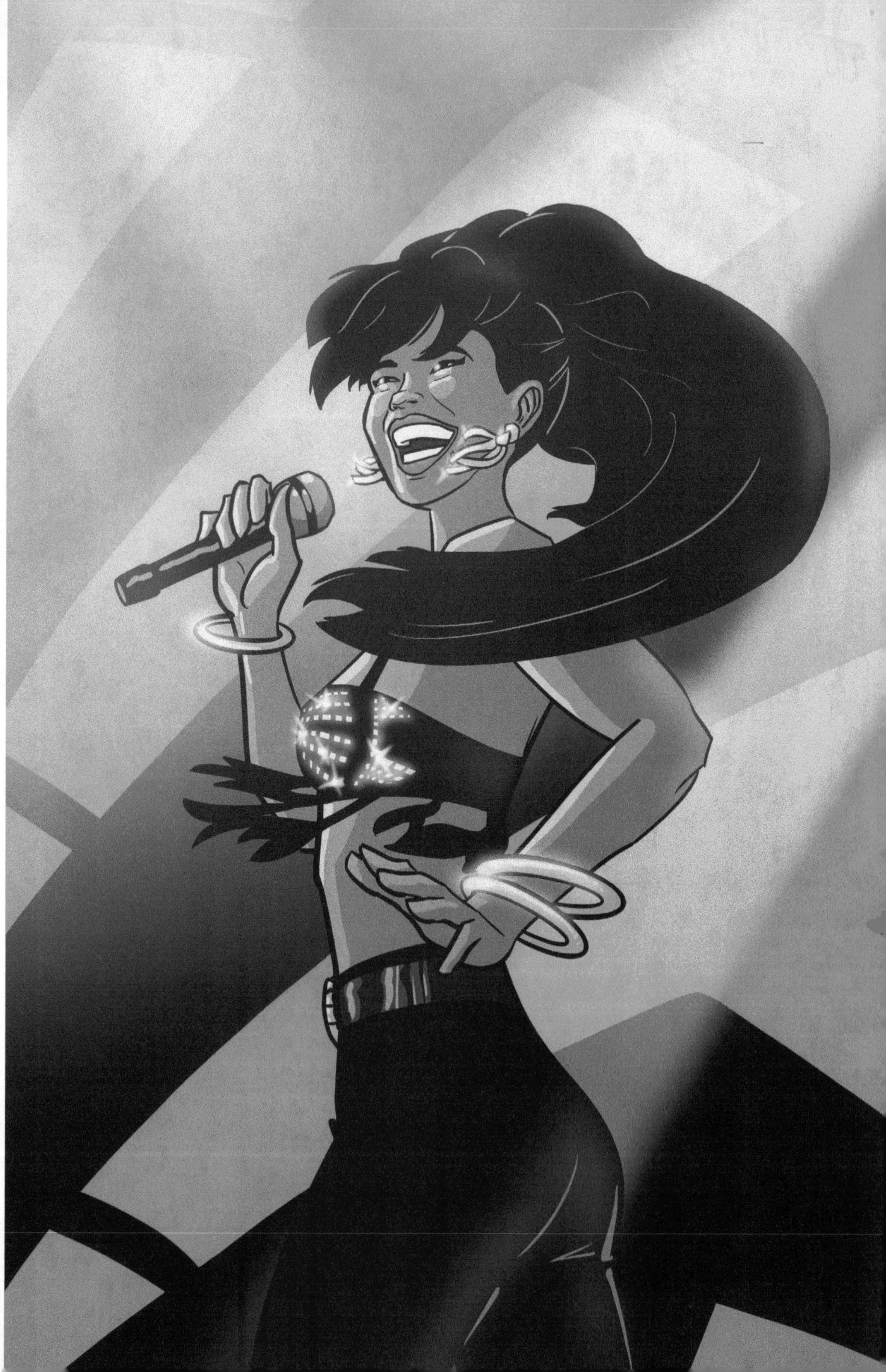